A
EUCHARISTIC
CHRISTMAS

Advent Meditations
on the Presence of Christ

SERVANT
BOOKS

PUBLISHED BY FRANCISCAN MEDIA
Cincinnati, Ohio

Cover and book design by Mark Sullivan
Cover image © PhotoXpress | ChantalS

LIBRARY OF CONGRESS CATALOGING-IN-PUBLICATION DATA
A Eucharistic Christmas : Advent meditations on the presence of Christ.
pages cm
ISBN 978-1-61636-808-1 (alk. paper)
1. Advent—Prayers and devotions. 2. Christmas—Prayers and devotions. 3. Lord›s Supper. I. Servant Books (Firm)
BV40.E825 2014
242'.33—dc23
2014016010

ISBN 978-1-61636-808-1

Published by Servant Books, an imprint of Franciscan Media
28 W. Liberty St.
Cincinnati, OH 45202
www.FranciscanMedia.org

Printed in the United States of America.
Printed on acid-free paper.
14 15 16 17 18 5 4 3 2 1

CONTENTS

God is not a theory! Christmas proves it. God is so real that we can taste and see his goodness (see Psalm 34). God's desire to dwell with us is not wishful thinking. He stands and knocks at the doors of our hearts. If we open our closed hearts to him, he comes in and has supper with us (see Revelation 3:20). In the Eucharist, Emmanuel—God with us—becomes a fact of our faith (see Matthew 1:23)

Unfortunately the depth of the Catholic Church's knowledge and teaching about the Eucharist too often falls on deaf or deadened ears. Statistics and expensive studies show that Catholics just don't fully grasp the greatest gift that God can give to his earthly Church: himself. We don't need an expensive study to prove what is already so obvious! Clearly reverence, respect, and devotion to the Eucharist diminishes with every generation.

But before you think I'm going to go on a rant about how bad everything is or how our Church is going to hell in a hand basket, I will take the advice I'd like to give you in this foreword. I will just shut up and sit in God's Eucharistic presence, soaking up the grace, and I will allow his words to formulate my reaction and responses to things that can frustrate me—especially in a season that's supposed to be joyful, but instead is filled with so much commercialism, rushing around, and materialism.

This book can help.

While it can be frustrating to see people so unaware that the Eucharist is the source of salvation, assigning blame doesn't get us (or our loved ones) to heaven. We need solutions! And the answer to these problems is discovered when the world lives the words of the song, "Silent Night"—that is, when we say nothing for a moment and just listen. "Be still, and know that I am God" (Psalm 46:10).

In this book we can enter more deeply into the true meaning of Christmas (which simply means "the sending of the Anointed One"). Each day we can take time to stop complaining and start contemplating. This book can be our daily companion to help incarnate the daily bread we receive at Mass. This collection of spiritual inspirations from some of our best contemporary spiritual writers can help us to prepare our hearts to celebrate with great anticipation all the gifts God wants to give to us.

As both a priest and chef, I have discovered true parallels in our faith through food—beginning with this holy season of Advent and Christmas. Consider how, in the city of Bethlehem ("House of Bread"), Mary placed Jesus in the manger (a place for animals to be fed). Consider that true peace happens when we turn our spears and swords into plowshares and pruning hooks (see Isaiah 2:4). Remember that the first to celebrate Christmas by adoring the Lamb of God who takes away our sins were shepherds (those who feed the flock). These connections, which fill our hunger for knowing God's love, can only come when we take time and marinate—that is, soak up—God's goodness through the ancient act of Eucharistic Adoration. Before our Lord, truly present in the Eucharist, we take in his goodness while hungering for the moment at Mass when we can be in fuller communion with him.

This book has great and balanced recipes to inspire us each day. It can certainly help us avoid a fast-food/fast-faith mentality and show us how to enjoy, relish, and savor this season of Advent waiting and Christmas feasting.

Faith, hope, love, peace, and joy are not mere theories. They are the facts of our faith. Christmas proves it. We just have to be hungry enough to take time and listen in the silence of that holy night.

With Mary's prayers and Christ's blessings,
—Fr. Leo E. Patalinghug, S.T.L.,
TV and radio host,
author of *Epic Food Fight*

Many years ago, when I was young and full of zeal, I said a prayer that changed my life. I told God that I would do anything he asked of me in order to set my spiritual life on fire. I thought the answer (if I even got one) would be something big and dramatic—maybe a forty-day fast, or a call to sell all my possessions. Instead, the answer came quickly and quietly in my heart: start going to Mass one day during the week. This simple direction started me on a lifelong love affair with Jesus in the Blessed Sacrament. This book is an invitation to enter more deeply into your own communion with Christ.

Why focus on the Eucharist at this busy time of year? During Advent we sing "O Come Emmanuel." We focus on the birth of Jesus, this innocent child who came into our world to be our savior. We think about the humanity of Jesus, his nearness to us. He is Emmanuel, God with us. But we can lose sight of the fact that God is with us always, particularly in his Eucharistic presence. The living, loving presence of Jesus is so available to us. We receive him at Sunday

Mass. We acknowledge his presence in the tabernacle. But for many of us, that's the end of it until the next Sunday.

The selections in this book invite us to go deeper. There are so many ways we can connect with Jesus. And he is eager for us to do just that. He offers a great gift by offering himself. At this time of year, we put a lot of energy into selecting just the right gifts to give those we love. We wrap them with care, and we feel happy when they are received with joy. The Eucharist is God's gift to us, and he is eager for us to receive his gift with joy.

This book covers the time from December 1 through the twelve days of Christmas, ending with January 6. Every day includes a simple meditation, a thought to help you respond, and a prayer to help you open your heart to his presence. Although the book centers on Jesus in the Blessed Sacrament, you may not be able to spend much time in a Church before his Eucharistic presence. But maybe you can go once for a time of Adoration. Maybe you can arrive a few minutes early for Sunday Mass. Certainly you can prepare your heart in a new way to receive him, and you can be more grateful for the gift of his presence as you come to understand better the greatness of the gift. Wherever you are when you read these meditations, you can put yourself spiritually in his presence and listen for his voice as he speaks to you.

May your celebration of Christmas this year bring you to the knowledge of God with us—and Jesus waiting for you in the Blessed Sacrament.

—Louise Paré

December 1
Prayer to Begin Eucharistic Adoration

Loving Father, your beloved Son has told us, "No one can come to me unless the Father who sent me draws him" (John 6:44). Thank you for drawing me here to the Eucharistic presence of Christ your Son. Thank you for allowing me to come close to the one who has come close to us in the Eucharist—who has become our companion on the way to you. Accept my sacrifice of prayer and the Adoration I offer to your Son in the Blessed Sacrament. Unworthy though I am, I come to behold Jesus Christ in this Sacrament of Charity, moved by the certainty that anyone who sees Jesus sees the Father. What impels me to this place is the same hunger that sent the starving prodigal son back to the embrace of his father. I come begging for a new beginning. Like those present at the feeding of the five thousand, I have nothing to offer you except my nothingness. But I look to your Son and join him in the thanks he offers to you. I come before the presence of your Son filled with an attitude of expectation. All my life, my heart has cried out with the psalmist, "Bow your heavens and come down!" (see Psalm 144:5). With unimaginable mercy you have answered that plea. I have been made for this presence. May I never be without wonder before the miracle of Jesus present in the Eucharist. Let me relive the surprise of the attraction of Christ. Give me eyes to see beyond all appearances. Make me attentive to the encounter you offer me in this sacrament. Please help me to offer this time of Adoration with all my heart, without becoming weary or distracted. United with the Mother of God, may I ardently adore the Fruit of Mary's womb so that my life may become fruitful in the way that best pleases you and that gives you unending glory. I ask this in the name of Jesus Christ our Lord. Amen.

—PETER JOHN CAMERON, O.P.

A THOUGHT FOR REFLECTION

Whether you are at home or praying before Jesus in the Blessed Sacrament, try to picture him in your mind as you pray these words. Think about the fact that he is drawing you to himself. Think about his desire to show himself to you. Think about the fact that he loves you, and ask him to help you experience his love. Then pray these words slowly, and let him speak to you personally. Linger over any words that strike you powerfully, and see how Jesus applies them to you.

Oh Jesus, present in the Blessed Sacrament,

Today I open my heart to your real presence and to the way you wish to speak to me. Teach me to listen and to be still so I can hear you. For these few minutes I put aside all the busyness of this season so I can focus on you. Thank you for the gift of your presence!

December 2
A Civilization of Love

The Christian mysteries exceed the capacities of human reason. We could never have discerned these truths if God had not revealed them to us. Ordinary language cannot do them justice. They strain even the specialized vocabularies of the sciences, such as philosophy and theology. They trespass far beyond the frontiers of poetry.

How then can we begin to speak of them?

Sciences falter and poetry fails, but love succeeds by grace. The love of Jesus impels the saints to awestruck silence but also to impassioned speech. It is Jesus whom the saints know in the Eucharist, the sacrament of the altar. There he is present, Body, Blood, soul, and divinity. Under the appearance of a small bit of bread, a drop of wine, God abides in his entirety. The finite contains all infinity, drawing us into communion, making us like himself, sharing his divine nature as generously as once he took up our human nature.

That infinite love is the power behind the words of the saints, the words of Catholics ancient and modern that appear in this book. The

Eucharist inspired them to extend the range of science and art, to elevate human words beyond their ordinary reach, to raise them to heaven, as the Eucharist raises the Church even now.

The Eucharist empowers Christians to build up new cultures on the ruins of the old ones. The Jewish historian Miri Rubin has demonstrated how the Church's profound belief in the real presence inspired the great achievements of the Middle Ages: the development of hospitals and universities, hospices and hostels. As the old Roman culture of death crumbled, Christians were able to build a civilization of love.

Through the Eucharist, God changes us as surely as he changed the elements of bread and wine into himself. He forms us as living stones in the temple of his Church. He builds up a Eucharistic culture to replace the culture of death.

Think globally? Act Eucharistically. It's the sacrament that renews the earth.

Asking what you can do for your country? Make a good Communion. Make a visit to the tabernacle. Much more will follow. God will make limitless poetry out of the prose of your life, and he will renew the face of the earth, beginning with your little corner.

—MIKE AQUILINA

A Thought for Reflection

Sometimes words fail us when we try to describe great truths, great moments, and great experiences in our lives. It is like that with the Eucharist. It is hard to wrap our minds around this mystery. Yet in our hearts we know that we are facing a truth too deep for words. "Act Eucharistically." What does that mean to you on a practical level?

Oh Jesus, present in the Blessed Sacrament,

I feel so small before your greatness. But something in me longs to understand you as much as I can. When my mind is too small to approach you, let my heart reach out to you. Take me one step closer to understanding you. Give me the gift of humility so I can approach you with simple faith.

DECEMBER 3
The Spiritual Hour of Power

Devotion to the Holy Eucharist is at the very heart of Catholic life. In his first message to the Church after his election, Pope Benedict XVI said that the Eucharist is "the heart of Christian life and the source of the Church's evangelizing mission."[1] As we know, Pope John Paul II also frequently emphasized the Church's Eucharist-centered spirituality. In fact, he died during the Year of the Eucharist, a time he had set aside for the Church to focus its attention on this sacrament, the center of our faith.

Every Catholic needs the vitality, wisdom, and strength that come forth from Jesus in the Holy Eucharist. Whether encountering the Lord for the first time in conversion, returning to the Lord after leaving the faith, or encountering him daily in faithful, ongoing conversion, every true Catholic will end up at the tabernacle.

---

1. First Message of His Holiness Benedict XVI at the End of the Eucharistic Concelebration with the Members of the College of Cardinals in the Sistine Chapel, April 20, 2005, http://www.vatican.va/holy_father/benedict_xvi/messages/pont-messages/2005/documents/hf_ben-xvi_mes_20050420_missa-pro-ecclesia_en.html, 4.

A Eucharistic holy hour is exactly as its name implies: an hour spent in prayer before Jesus in the tabernacle. Archbishop Fulton J. Sheen was one of the twentieth century's greatest apologists and evangelists, as well as the National Director of the Society for the Propagation of the Faith for sixteen years. He was so convinced of the importance of the Eucharistic holy hour for his life and ministry that he made a holy hour daily for over fifty years, despite a demanding schedule and worldwide travel. He called it, fittingly, the "hour of power."

A former secretary of the archbishop's told me that he always made his holy hour after breakfast. (Archbishop Sheen once said that people should never try to make a holy hour before they've had their first cup of coffee!) He then spent additional time near the chapel writing, drawing his inspiration from our Lord in the Eucharist. When people congratulated him for his fine speaking and writing, telling him that he was very talented, he always answered that he had no such talent. He said that the power of his words, written and spoken, came from Jesus in the Blessed Sacrament.

—Andrew Apostoli, C.F.R.

A Thought for Reflection

Don't let the idea of a holy hour intimidate you. Spend whatever time you have. Place yourself spiritually before the Blessed Sacrament, no matter where you are praying. How can you work some regular time for Adoration into your schedule?

Oh Jesus, present in the Blessed Sacrament,

Bring me into this process of conversion so I can become more like you. Take my weariness and distraction and replace it with your power and overflowing goodness. Transform my thinking so I can respond out of your power. Fill me with your vitality, wisdom, and strength.

December 4
Talk to Jesus

Pope Benedict XVI touched upon the littleness with which we must enter into the mystery of the self-gift of Jesus in the Eucharist when he spoke to the College of Cardinals the day after his election.

> The Eucharist makes constantly present the Risen Christ who continues to give himself to us, calling us to participate in the banquet of his Body and his Blood. From full communion with him flows every other element of the Church's life; first of all, communion among all the faithful, the commitment to proclaiming and witnessing to the Gospel, the ardor of love for all, especially the poorest and lowliest.[2]

---

2. First Message of His Holiness Benedict XVI at the End of the Eucharistic Concelebration with the Members of the College of Cardinals in the Sistine Chapel, April 20, 2005, http://www.vatican.va/holy_father/benedict_xvi/messages/pont-messages/2005/documents/hf_ben-xvi_mes_20050420_missa-pro-ecclesia_en.html, 4.

Yes, Jesus has truly become that intimate with us. He has given himself as our food and drink. His celebration of the Eucharist is our reception of love himself, our receiving his flesh and blood into our flesh and blood.

At Mass do we really take the opportunity to talk to Christ? Is there any more intimate moment to do this than upon receiving him in the Eucharist? If we miss the intimacy of receiving him who has given himself completely to us, we fail to draw upon the power that lies right under our noses, right in our own tradition. The Church gives us many avenues toward peace and intimacy, but we find it especially in the sacramental intimacy with the Lord that we have in the Eucharist.

Rather than spending our days rushing about, nervously talking to ourselves about what is going on or going wrong, let's take the opportunity to deepen our communion with the Lord whom we have received in Holy Communion. This ongoing communion with the Lord takes our prayer into a real relationship.

This may sound pious, but try it. We can have the fruit of union with Jesus and can continue with him personally in words or in wordless love rather than just thinking about him or forgetting about him altogether. It might seem impossible because of all our obligations and preoccupations and our tendency to become absorbed in them.

It might seem that it would require enormous willpower and self-discipline, which I know I lack. But for God all things are possible.

—Thomas Acklin, O.S.B.

A Thought for Reflection

There are a million reasons to be distracted when we receive Communion. But what an opportunity we miss! Receiving Communion is really entering into communion with Jesus—it's not just an action; it is a key part of a relationship. This Advent when you go to Mass, try to spend a few minutes beforehand thinking of what you are about to do. More specifically, think about who you are going to receive. Jesus's Body becomes part of your body. What does that mean to you?

Oh Jesus, present in the Blessed Sacrament,

I'm sorry for the many distractions that have kept me from receiving you worthily in the past. I pray that your Holy Spirit will teach me more about this sacrament. Help me to think about you during the week and to look forward to this time of communion with you. I can hardly begin to understand the degree of union you want with me—body and soul. But I want to learn.

December 5
Transformation

L ike Mary, our mother, we have been called by God to bring the
life of Jesus Christ to the world. And like our mother, we, too,
must be impregnated by the spirit of the Gospel, imbued by the one
whose name is Jesus Christ. We have considered the supreme degree
to which our Holy Mother, assimilated to the Word of God, became
a reflection of him whom she bore. She models for us the degree of
transformation to which each of us is called.

Prayer, obedience, and acting with the wisdom of God lead us on
the path of transformation. But it is when we receive into our bodies
the one whose image we wish to reflect that we are most powerfully
transformed. As Mary conceived Jesus in the confines of her body,
we, too, are to conceive him in the wombs of our hearts. Through the
gift of the Eucharist, we receive the very person of Jesus Christ, and
in so doing become a chalice of his life.

To the extent we receive the Eucharist with faith and conviction and adore the heart of our Lord as given to us in the Blessed

Sacrament, we encourage the transformation process God has begun in us. Pope Paul VI tells us that "anyone who approaches this august sacrament with special devotion…experiences how great is the value of communing with Christ…for there is nothing more effective for advancing on the road to holiness."[3] At every moment of the day, throughout the world, Jesus offers himself to us in the form of bread and wine so that we might be nourished with his own Body and Blood. And we, suffering from spiritual blindness, do not recognize him in the breaking of the bread.

Authentic catechesis on the real presence has been absent from many religion classes for many years. This omission spans catechetical instruction from elementary schools to seminary courses. Many people under the age of forty have never been to any form of Eucharistic Adoration. However, they are not to be blamed. They only need to be instructed so that the spiritual benefits of the Eucharist can become a transforming agent in their lives.

—Johnnette Benkovic

---

3. *Mysterium Fides*, 69.

A Thought for Reflection

The idea of personal transformation is very attractive until we actually begin to experience being transformed. Then we discover how attached we are to our own way of thinking and acting. As we get closer to Jesus in the Eucharist, he will begin to transform us—we will become more like him. Do you want to let him get that close to you? It will mean changing, which requires humility. Ask him for the grace of this transformation to begin working in your heart.

Oh Jesus, present in the Blessed Sacrament,

It fills me with awe as I begin to understand the truth of you living in me. I want to become more like you in my thoughts and my actions. In this very busy time of year, help me to be patient and to put the needs of others before my own. As I experience your love for me more deeply, let me love others out of the strength of that love. I surrender to you.

December 6
A Window into Heaven

A *men* is our response to the person who administers the Blessed Sacrament to us. It comes from the Hebrew term for truth. So we are saying, "In truth, I believe this is the Body of Christ."

Hence we are not saying "amen" to a mere symbol. No, our amen is the response of faith to Christ's own words: "This is my body.…This is my blood" (see Matthew 26:26–29). It brings us up, so to speak, to Christ's level of commitment, of meaning, of sincerity in what he says and does.

Such is the loving commitment of Jesus to us; such is his desire to be with us; such is his desire that we should be with him. Our amen reaches much deeper, however, because the sacrament of the Eucharist invites us much deeper.

At its minimum, this is the sacrament of the physical proximity of Jesus to us. It is the sacrament of Christ's fidelity to the incarnation of his divine person. It is the memorial of the extremity of love with which he loved us.

We may stretch our eyesight through telescopes or other instruments as far as the outer galaxies to see if we can catch a glimpse of him at the right hand of the Father. But he has chosen a far better way, a way that permits him to be with the Father, and yet to be with us. That way is the Eucharist, God still among us, always among us until the end of the age.

And in that sacramental Body—which we contemplate momentarily in our hand, or on our tongue, or more at length behind the tabernacle door or exposed in the monstrance—we are not seeing a symbol. The Eucharist is like a window into heaven itself, a window that becomes ever more transparent the more we allow the Body of the Lord to become our own body, the more we allow our own bodies to become his. We commune with him in Communion so as to be transformed into him as he is being transformed into us.

This is the grace of the Eucharist: communion, becoming more fully one body with the Lord and with one another. That is why *the Eucharist creates the Church*, and the Church, in witnessing to the Body of the Lord, draws people toward him.

—PETER MAGEE

A Thought for Reflection

Our amen when we receive Communion is an affirmation that we are truly receiving the living Jesus and that we are physically united with him in this sacrament. The next time you receive Communion, think more deeply about what it means to say "amen."

Oh Jesus, present in the Blessed Sacrament,

Give me greater faith that it is truly your Body and Blood that I receive. Where I lack faith, increase my belief in your real presence. Amen. I believe in you.

Grace

How do we receive grace? There are three major avenues. First of all, we can receive grace through some form of prayer: prayer of blessing and adoration, prayer of petition, intercessory prayer, prayer of thanksgiving, or prayer of praise. Likewise, it can be any expression of prayer: vocal prayer, meditation, contemplative prayer, community prayer, liturgical prayer, or psalm prayer.

The second major source of that spiritual energy we call grace comes from practicing the virtues, such as faith, hope, charity, prudence, justice, fortitude, and temperance. In fact, some fifty-six virtues have been catalogued over the years. (Even suffering could be considered a virtue when it is motivated by love, since it could be a manifestation of the virtues of fortitude, perseverance, mortification, temperance, and self-control.)

The third source of grace is the seven sacraments. Of the seven sacraments, only two—the sacraments of reconciliation (penance) and the Eucharist—may be received frequently. And of the seven, the Eucharist is the greatest source of grace. When we receive the Eucharist, we receive not only grace but the very Author of Grace; in receiving the Eucharist, we do not receive a *thing* but God himself in his human nature as Christ and his divine nature as God. Consequently, the Eucharist transcends any other source of grace, and as St. Thomas Aquinas asserts, it is the ultimate focal point of all the other sacraments.

We can attain great holiness by prayer alone. We can also attain advanced holiness by practicing any one of the virtues, since the full spectrum of virtue grows, as St. Thomas Aquinas explains, the way the hand grows—not one finger at a time but all together. As one finger grows, the other fingers grow simultaneously. Likewise, as we practice any one virtue, the other virtues will grow too. But when it comes to maximizing our holiness, nothing exceeds the sacraments as a source of grace. The seven sacraments are designed by God to be the main avenues of our encounter with him, and among the sacraments, the Eucharist is the greatest in terms of conferring grace and having the power to make us holy.

—JOHN HAMPSCH, C.M.F.

A Thought for Reflection

Grace is defined as an unmerited gift from God, something he gives us freely, not because we earned it. Grace helps us grow in virtue and holiness. Ask Jesus for an increase of grace as you receive him in Holy Communion.

Oh Jesus, present in the Blessed Sacrament,

> I open my heart to receive your grace in this sacrament. Although I am unworthy, I believe you are purifying me and bringing me closer to you. Thank you for the free gift of your grace.

THE ANNUNCIATION

B eing Christian is not the result of an ethical choice or a lofty idea. Being Christian is the result of an encounter with a person. That encounter begins when the Blessed Virgin Mary pronounces her yes to the archangel and the Word of God becomes flesh in her womb. Salvation becomes a real presence in the world that we can encounter in a human way. Since the time of the psalmist we have begged the Lord to lower his heavens and come down to us. Thanks to the obedience of the Blessed Virgin, that has happened. The encounter that begins at the Annunciation remains the method that God uses to draw all people to him. It finds its source and summit in the celebration of the Eucharist. At Mass we are like Mary before the angel: We wait for Christ's flesh and blood to inhabit bread and wine. Expecting, we wait for our lives to change.

The Visitation

The Blessed Virgin Mary's journey from Nazareth to the town in Judah where Elizabeth lived was the first Corpus Christi procession. The Mother of God comes to her kinswoman bearing in her womb the Word become flesh. Mary makes her way to her cousin—and to all of us—in order to place in front of us the mystery that puts to flight all our fear, all our negativity, all our hopelessness. When Elizabeth encounters the presence of Christ in the womb of Mary, the child in her own womb leaps for joy. So too, the power of the real presence in the Eucharist has the power to reach past all our resistance, all our impenetrability and inflame us with new purpose, certainty, and gladness. Pope Benedict XVI says that the feast of Corpus Christi is an expression of faith in the fact that God is love. We welcome Mary so that we can be confirmed in that fact.

—PETER JOHN CAMERON, O.P.

A Thought for Reflection

As we go though our busy preparations for Christmas, we remember that Mary was also busy, preparing for the birth of her child and visiting her relatives. She had a lot to ponder, wondering what it would mean to give birth to the Messiah. We wonder also about this child and the importance of our faith response to his coming. Ask Mary to help you believe and respond to her Son.

Oh Jesus, present in the Blessed Sacrament,

> Mary responded wholeheartedly to your invitation to bear you in her womb. In a similar way you ask me to bring you into the world by my love and actions toward others. Like Mary, I am in awe of your invitation. And like Mary, I say yes to you. Let your will be done now and always.

Jesus Feeds Us

A s is often the case in Holy Scripture, when God intends to do something extraordinary, he prepares his people for it by revealing beforehand what he is about to do. Here, Jesus was about to tell the people that he intended to give them his Body and Blood as food for their souls. He was about to reveal to them the new and amazing doctrine of the real presence. So he prepared them for hearing this mysterious teaching by working a truly astounding miracle.

St. John situates this miracle at the time of the Jewish feast of the Passover. A large crowd was following Jesus, drawn by the fact that he was healing so many people. Jesus knew the people would be hungry. St. John tells us that Jesus already knew what he was going to do, but he decided to test his disciple, Philip, and asked him, "Where can we buy enough food for them to eat?" Poor Philip could not even begin to think of a way to feed such a crowd! He pointed out to Jesus that it would take two hundred days' wages to buy enough food to feed everyone even a minimal amount of food. Suddenly, a small boy approached Jesus and his apostles, offering them five small barley loaves and two small fish. Certainly this meager offering appeared rather pitiful because even the apostle Andrew remarked, "What good are these for so many?" Nonetheless, Jesus had all the people recline so they could eat. We know what happened next: "Taking the five loaves and the two fish he looked up to heaven, and blessed, and broke and gave the loaves to the disciples, and the disciples gave them to the crowds." (Matthew 14:19). Everyone ate until they were satisfied. Jesus then instructed the disciples to collect the food that was left over. When they did, they had twelve baskets full of fragments from the five barley loaves. Having witnessed this miracle, the crowd was so awestruck they wanted to take Jesus by force and make him their king. However, Jesus perceived this and fled.

—JOHN HAMPSCH, C.M.F.

A THOUGHT FOR REFLECTION

Maybe if we witnessed a miracle like the feeding of five thousand people, it would be easier for us to believe in the gift of the Eucharist. The words of consecration at every Mass bring about a quiet miracle. Bread and wine become the Body and Blood of Jesus. Do you believe in this great miracle?

Oh Jesus, present in the blessed sacrament,

I believe that you are truly present, Body and Blood, soul and divinity, in the Blessed Sacrament. Where my faith is weak, give me the gift of greater faith. Because I believe in your true presence, I bow before you and worship you.

December 10
A Sneak Preview of the Eucharist

U ndoubtedly, Jesus fed the people because they were hungry. But it also seems clear that this was an ideal opportunity to give his followers an image of the sacrament he would formally institute one year later at the Last Supper. How do we see the Eucharist prefigured in this miracle? The imagery is powerful and overwhelming!

First of all, the miracle takes place "as the Passover draws near," the same time of the year that Jesus would later choose to institute the Eucharist. The proximity of this feast certainly must have evoked images of Moses among the people in the crowd. As we shall see later, the Gospel writers capitalize on this imagery to portray Jesus as the new Moses. For example, Jesus ascended a mountain before feeding the people miraculous bread, just as Moses ascended a mountain before supplying the Israelites with manna as they wandered in the desert.

Second, Jesus uses the same sequence of actions here that he repeats at the Last Supper: He takes the bread, blesses it, and distributes it to his disciples, who in turn give it to the people.

Third, Jesus's blessing of the bread has supernatural power in both instances. In this case, the bread is miraculously multiplied to feed five thousand men. At the Last Supper, Jesus miraculously changes ordinary bread and wine into his Body and Blood.

Fourth, Jesus provides his followers with all the material sustenance they need at the miracle of the loaves and fishes. In fact, the Gospels tell us the people ate until they were full, and an abundant surplus of twelve full baskets still remained. In the Eucharist, Jesus provides us with all the spiritual sustenance we need to live for him. We can receive the Eucharist fully expecting that Christ will give us spiritual life through it. Moreover, Christ is not stingy; his provision for us is abundant. Not only will he take care of our spiritual needs, but we can also trust he will take care of our material needs as well (metaphorically expressed in the phrase "our daily bread").

—JOHN HAMPSCH, C.M.F.

A THOUGHT FOR REFLECTION

The Eucharist is the daily bread for our souls. Consider going to Mass an extra day during the week if your schedule allows. When you are not able to attend Mass, put yourself spiritually in Christ's presence and ask him to give you the grace of his presence. Jesus gives us all the food we need to satisfy the hunger of our hearts, but it's our choice whether or not to receive him.

Oh Jesus, present in the Blessed Sacrament,
I humbly ask you to feed my soul, to satisfy the desires of my heart, and to unite me to you in this holy sacrament. I invite you into my soul and I thank you for coming near to me.

DECEMBER 11
Introduce Jesus to Others

Pope Benedict XVI, you will recall, stated that the Eucharist is "the source of the Church's evangelizing mission." Since this is the case, what will the hour of power do for us as we try to bring the Good News to those around us?

Time spent before the Eucharist deepens our personal encounter with Christ himself. He becomes more real to us and our faith increases. This is important for evangelization because faith has two critical elements, belief and trust. Faith is the "the conviction of things not seen" (Hebrews 11:1). We do not see Christ in the Holy Eucharist with the eyes of our body, but with the eyes of faith: We know and believe he is really present, Body, Blood, soul, and divinity. To paraphrase St. Thomas Aquinas's beautiful hymn, "Tantum Ergo," faith will tell us Christ is present when our human senses fail.

Regarding trust, faith is "the assurance of things hoped for" (Hebrews 11:1). Once our faith moves us to believe in Jesus's real presence in the Blessed Sacrament, we also experience a growing desire for others to love him, even the whole world. Like St. Andrew, after our personal stay with Jesus, we will lose no time going out to bring family, friends, strangers, and yes, even enemies of the Church, to Jesus.

None of us can introduce someone to a person we don't know or can't find. If we are rooted in Eucharistic devotion, we know who Jesus is and where we can always find him. As someone once put it, the measure of our holiness and effectiveness with others is the degree in which God becomes real in our lives. Where can Jesus become more real for us than in the Blessed Sacrament?

When we are before our Eucharistic Lord, we should ask that he anoint our words, written and spoken, so that they convey the convincing power of the Spirit and not simply the wisdom of men (see 1 Corinthians 2:4–5). Furthermore, we must plead with Jesus so that those we evangelize are disposed to receive him, his message, and his Church.

—ANDREW APOSTOLI, C.F.R.

A THOUGHT FOR REFLECTION

The best way to get to know someone is to spend time with them. As the disciples spent time with Jesus in his daily life, so we are able to spend time with him in the Eucharist. He is the same now as he was when he walked on the earth. The more we get to know him, the more we can help others get to know him.

Oh Jesus, present in the Blessed Sacrament,

I'd like to be your friend, to know you and to have you know me. I bring all my relationships and desires and responsibilities to you in prayer because I want you to be involved in all these everyday experiences of my life.

DECEMBER 12
Think about Jesus

There is much to adore in the Body of the Lord. As you allow your eyes to become fixed upon that little white host, think of the eternity that lies behind it. Think of the vast universe, which sooner or later will be drawn into that host, for judgment unto life or death.

Think of the body of him who was truly born of the Virgin Mary. Think of all he went through as a child, an adolescent, a youth, a young adult—like us in every way except sin.

Think of the hands that blessed the children and healed the sick, of the voice that calmed the storm and called Lazarus from the tomb; of the eyes that pierced with love the heart of the rich young man, that saw Nathaniel and Matthew from a distance before calling them to leave everything and follow him.

Think of those feet that walked mile after mile to preach the Good News of salvation; "God is with you, for *I* am with you!" Think of his smile, his singing voice, his angry and majestic voice, his tearful cries, his gentle whispering.

Think, finally, of his passion and of the marks it made on his body, those same marks that are now glorified, that we now receive in the sacrament of the Eucharist and that one day we shall behold with our own eyes if we live and die in his love.

As your heart is drawn into his through contemplation of the Eucharist, draw to your own heart the millions of people suffering in millions of ways. For them, the Body of the Lord will be their eternal healing and salvation.

Remember those who curse him, reject him, despise him. Allow your own heart to feel something of his pain. Perhaps God will use your life to draw some of them to bless, accept, and adore him.

Pope John Paul II calls the Eucharist the "heart of the world."[4] Who among us does not want to say *amen* to that, to be in, to bear with, that heart? Let our resounding amen lead us to seek time to love and adore him in the Eucharist. Let us come to understand deeply how the heart of Jesus beats with eternal, crazy love for this passing, crazy world in which we are but pilgrims.

—PETER MAGEE

4. *Ecclesia de Eucharistia*, "On the Eucharist in its Relationship to the Church," 59.

A Thought for Reflection

During December we think about the birth of Christ and his human life. He is Emmanuel, God with us. When we pray in the presence of the Blessed Sacrament, he is there in the fullness of his divinity and his humanity, for these two natures are inseparable. What can you learn about Jesus through his fully human and fully divine nature?

Oh Jesus, present in the Blessed Sacrament,

> I set aside my own understanding and ask you to reveal to me the wonder of your incarnation. You are God, wholly divine and wholly human. Because of this I have hope of sharing in your divine life for all eternity. Thank you for the great hope you give, that I will be united to you forever.

DECEMBER 13
Holy Hour Inspiration

Bishop Fulton J. Sheen is the person who seems to have popularized the Eucharistic holy hour in this country. He was asked shortly before he died in 1979 what had inspired him to take up this practice. His answer was surprising. He said it was a young Chinese girl, age eleven.

When the Communists took power in China, they made a certain priest a prisoner in his own house. He was able to see the church from his window. He saw the Communists break open the tabernacle and throw the ciborium down with all the hosts spilling out on the floor. The priest had counted the hosts: there were thirty-two.

A little girl had seen this as she prayed in the back of the church. That night, and for thirty-one more nights, she came back, snuck by the guards and prayed before the hosts for an hour to make reparation for the terrible desecration of the Eucharist. Each night at the end of the hour, she would lean down and receive a host with her tongue, since at that time a layperson could not take the host in the hand.

On the last night, when she had received the last host, one of the guards saw her leave. He followed her and beat her to death. The priest watched this in horror.

When Fulton Sheen heard this story, he was so moved that he resolved to spend one hour each day of his priesthood before the Blessed Sacrament. And, of course, by his talks, given all over the world, he inspired many others to do the same.

As Bishop Sheen pointed out, the holy hour is one of the few direct requests our blessed Lord made of his apostles: "Could you not watch with me one hour?" (Matthew 26:40). It is my hope that the example of that little Chinese girl and of Bishop Sheen will inspire many reading this to do the same. Spend an hour in Adoration of our Eucharistic Lord each day.

—THOMAS G. MORROW

A THOUGHT FOR REFLECTION

The girl in this story had no problem with faith in Jesus's real presence in the Blessed Sacrament. And she risked her life to honor and serve him. As adults we can lose the simplicity of faith that this girl demonstrated. How can you express your faith and love to him?

Oh Jesus, present in the Blessed Sacrament,

The faith of this young girl inspires me and inflames my heart. Give me that kind of love and devotion. Make me more willing to sacrifice my time, my other priorities, and the control of my life. Above all, teach me to love you as you love me.

DECEMBER 14
"I Am the Bread of Life"

Jesus said to them, "I am the bread of life; he who comes to me shall not hunger, and he who believes in me shall never thirst. But I said to you that you have seen me and yet do not believe. All that the Father gives me will come to me; and him who comes to me I will not cast out. For I have come down from heaven, not to do my own will, but the will of him who sent me; and this is the will of him who sent me, that I should lose nothing of all that he has given me, but raise it up at the last day. For this is the will of my Father, that every one who sees the Son and believes in him should have eternal life; and I will raise him up at the last day."

The Jews then murmured at him, because he said, "I am the bread which came down from heaven." They said, "Is not this Jesus, the son of Joseph, whose father and mother we know? How does he now say, 'I have come down from heaven'?" Jesus answered them, "Do not murmur among yourselves. No one can come to me unless the Father who sent me draws him; and I will raise him up at the last day. It is written in the prophets, 'And they shall all be taught by God.' Every one who has heard and learned from the Father comes to me. Not that any one has seen the Father except him who is from God; he has seen the Father. Truly, truly, I say to you, he who believes has eternal life. I am the bread of life. Your fathers ate the manna in the wilderness, and they died. This is the bread which comes down from heaven, that a man may eat of it and not die. I am the living bread which came down from heaven; if any one eats of this bread, he will live for ever; and the bread which I shall give for the life of the world is my flesh."

The Jews then disputed among themselves, saying, "How can this man give us his flesh to eat?" So Jesus said to them, "Truly, truly, I say to you, unless you eat the flesh of the Son of man and drink his blood, you have no life in you; he who eats my flesh and drinks my blood has eternal life, and I will raise him up at the last day. For my flesh is food indeed, and my blood is drink indeed. He who eats my flesh and drinks my blood abides in me, and I in him. As the living Father sent me, and I live because of the Father, so he who eats me will live because of me. This is the bread which came down from heaven, not such as the fathers ate and died; he who eats this bread will live for ever." This he said in the synagogue, as he taught at Capernaum.

—JOHN 6:35–59

A Thought for Reflection

Jesus said of himself that he was the Bread of Life. Bread is a source of sustenance for our bodies. In this sacrament Jesus is the sustenance of our souls. In what ways does Jesus sustain you?

Oh Jesus, present in the Blessed Sacrament,

> Let your holy words penetrate my heart. Speak to me through the Scriptures. I long for your living bread.

DECEMBER 15
God's Great Gift to Us

St. Augustine, the great saint who lived in the fourth century and was converted from his worldly ways through the unceasing prayers of his mother, St. Monica, once launched a spiritual teaching with what today's advertising moguls would call a "teaser." He said, "There is only one thing God does not know. He does not know how he could give us a gift greater than himself—and he has given us the gift of himself as bread in the Holy Eucharist."

We know that God is omniscient; he knows everything. Yet, it seems that in giving us the ultimate gift of himself in the Eucharist, God has exhausted his divine ingenuity. The gift of himself is not merely a spiritual gift, or charism. It is not even simply offering himself as a friend to us. Rather, God gives himself to us in the closest kind of intimacy—physically and spiritually—in the union called Communion.

Communion involves a physical, spiritual, and emotional intimacy in which God, whom the heavens cannot contain, is totally contained within our heart and our body. This is a supernal marvel that only God could design. It is as if God's limitless love has, as it were, exhausted his own divine ingenuity in designing a way to get eminently close to his beloved human creatures, whom he has fashioned in his own image and likeness.

How little we appreciate this marvelous plan of God. How seldom we are thankful for it. How rarely we avail ourselves of God's gift to us, not only in terms of frequency but also in terms of fervor.

This classic Augustinian insight—that God does not know how to give us a gift greater than himself—should alert us to the fact that this greatest gift is accompanied by incredible power. When the supreme gift is fully embraced by a human heart bursting with love, this power is available to us.

—JOHN HAMPSCH, C.M.F.

A THOUGHT FOR REFLECTION

If God has given us such an overwhelming gift, what gift can we give him in return? Is there something you hesitate to surrender to him? Is there some fear that holds you back? Give him your heart, the gift he has been waiting for.

Oh Jesus, present in the Blessed Sacrament,

Jesus, thank you for the gift of yourself, a grace I can hardly imagine. I offer you the gift of my heart, purified by your precious Blood. I can't match the magnificence of your gift, but I give you all I am in faith and humility. Thank you for desiring this gift.

DECEMBER 16
Connected to the Power Source

Jesus's parable of the sower (see Matthew 13:1–9; 18–23) compares the human heart to soil that received the planter's seed. Some of the seed falls on the path and the birds eat it; some falls on rocky ground and springs up quickly but just as quickly dies for lack of roots; some falls among thorns and is choked off; some falls on good soil. Using this parable as a guide, we should ask Jesus to open the hearts of those who are closed or resistant because they lack understanding (the path souls), to strengthen the hearts of those who are weak and inconsistent (the rocky souls), and to set free those held back by sinful attachments and addictions (the thorn souls). The seed has potential for a tremendous yield—as much as a hundredfold—but the soil where it lands makes all the difference.

Fulton Sheen used to say the hour of power drives from our hearts any spiritual mediocrity, laziness, indifference, and fear. The life of love in the Eucharistic heart of Jesus will set our own hearts on fire with ardent love for him. Then we will go with courage and conviction to bring the whole world to Jesus. Then will Jesus's desire come closer to fulfillment. "I came to cast fire upon the earth; and would that it were already kindled!" (Luke 12:49).

Jesus told St. Faustina that there are two thrones of his mercy in the world: the tabernacle and the confessional. Jesus in the Eucharist sustains us in our daily lives and also sustains our work of evangelization by equipping us with the power of the Holy Spirit. Just as a power tool disconnected from its power source won't work, so the Catholic disconnected from the Eucharistic Lord becomes ineffective. Countless demands and activities of all sorts sweep us along so that we easily become disconnected from the Lord. He will daily recharge the batteries of our life and ministry during the hour of power. As we pray before the tabernacle and maintain our living relationship with Jesus, we will find ourselves abundantly blessed and better able to communicate God's mercy to a broken world.

—ANDREW APOSTOLI, C.F.R.

A THOUGHT FOR REFLECTION

Two sacraments, penance and the Eucharist, connect us to God's mercy. This mercy is not just for us, but for all the world. The season of Advent is an excellent time to go to confession. Have you been recently? If not, what is holding you back?

Oh Jesus, present in the Blessed Sacrament,

I know that I have sinned and wounded my relationship with you and with others. Have mercy on me, and forgive my sins. Let me be a sign of your love to all that I meet, as I experience your merciful love here in your holy presence.

December 17
Believe

I f we are to reap the fullness of grace that the Eucharist offers us, then we must first believe that we are receiving the Body and Blood of our Lord Jesus Christ. To fortify our own belief, or to help those who do not believe, we should know what Jesus Himself tells us about the gift he offers.

Reading the sixth chapter of the Gospel of John (verses 25–71), we discover that the crisis of faith surrounding the real presence is not new. In fact, it caused the first division in the body of Christ. Here Jesus referred to himself as the Bread of Life: "I am the living bread which came down from heaven; if any one eats of this bread, he will live for ever; and the bread which I shall give for the life of the world is my flesh" (John 6:51). Finding this a hard teaching, the disciples murmured among themselves, asking one another, "How can this man give us his flesh to eat?"

At these words the Jews grew angry, and their murmurs broke into quarreling. Jesus responded, "Truly, truly I say to you, unless you eat the flesh of the Son of man and drink his blood, you have no life in you…. For my flesh is food indeed, and my blood is drink indeed. He who eats my flesh and drinks my blood abides in me and I in him" (John 6:53, 55–56). So that there could not be any doubt to what he meant, Jesus emphasized this statement by saying, "Truly, truly, I say to you," over and over again (John 6:26, 32, 47, 53).

The belief that Jesus Christ is truly and substantially present in the Eucharist is a sign of true discipleship. In the closing verses of John 6, Peter demonstrated this mark of being the true disciple when he responded to Jesus's question. As the unbelieving disciples walked away, Jesus turned to the twelve and asked, "Will you also go away?" Simon Peter responded, "Lord, to whom shall we go? You have the words of eternal life; and we have believed, and have come to know that you are the Holy One of God" (John 6: 67–69).

May we, like Peter, be true disciples who acknowledge Jesus Christ, truly present in the Eucharist, and may we, like Peter, express our confidence in him to others.

—Johnnette Benkovic

A Thought for Reflection

Jesus's teaching on the Eucharist caused division right from the start. Many stopped following him because of it. Do you believe that the bread and wine become the Body and Blood of Jesus? Do you believe it is truly Jesus that we receive? Are you willing to defend this truth to others?

Oh Jesus, present in the Blessed Sacrament,

With Peter I pray, "Lord, to whom would I go except to you? You have the words of everlasting life." Even when my understanding is weak, I hold on to you with faith and with love. Give me greater faith so I will never doubt you or turn my back on you.

December 18
Spending Time Alone with Jesus

("Paula" answers questions from a Catholic journalist about her experience in Eucharistic Adoration.)

What was it like when you first started to experience the real presence of Christ in Eucharistic Adoration?

It's so much easier to talk about the miraculous and earth-shattering things; it's much harder to describe the more subtle things that happen in Adoration. It would be like trying to describe the love and the security you have, and somewhat take for granted, in your family and closest friends. You could tell people what you do for and with one another, and you'd tend to talk about the big things—birthday parties, Christmas presents, vacations together, whatever—but the relationship, the bond itself, isn't moving from one big thing to the next. It's really in countless little moments. It's in the trust, sensitivity, and caring you have for each other. And that's more what the experience of Adoration is like, for me at least. Yes, there are the big moments. But they're relatively few. The little moments of peace, just being still and knowing he is God—that's really the fountain that you're drinking from in Adoration.

Did you read Scripture and spiritual books to help increase your awareness of his presence?

Yes. A lot. One of the books I read very early on was a collection of letters from one priest to a brother priest. I don't remember the title, but the letters were about Eucharistic Adoration. And the things that he said in there—a lot of them were quotes from saints and modern holy people like Mother Teresa—he would talk about Jesus being so happy to see us when we come in to adore him. "Jesus is smiling," he said, "just overjoyed to see us coming to be with him." That book helped put me at ease; it put holy thoughts and images in my mind, and that helped me very much with my prayer. It made it much easier to pray in the Adoration chapel. Remember: I was very nervous about the whole thing at first, very afraid I would do something wrong in there.

—QUOTED BY DAVID PEARSON

A Thought for Reflection

Paula learned to overcome her nervousness about spending time alone in Adoration. It's normal to feel nervous at first, but as the relationship deepens, the nervousness goes away. Paula did a lot of reading for inspiration. What can you do to be more comfortable when you are alone with Jesus?

Oh Jesus, present in the Blessed Sacrament,

Help me overcome any fear I have of you or of being in silence. Help me remember how much you love me, how much you desire this time together, and how close you are to me in this sacrament. You are my Emmanuel, God with me. Thank you for coming so close to me.

DECEMBER 19
The Eucharistic Imagination of Jesus

From the first instant that Jesus Christ came to be in the womb of the Blessed Virgin Mary, the Lord began to live his final promise: "I am with you always" (Matthew 28:20). Throughout his life on Earth, Jesus prepared for the everlasting presence he would offer us in the Eucharist. The Lord's forty-day fast in the desert taught him firsthand that to be human means being hungry and thirsty. We starve for truth and meaning; we thirst for what will totally satisfy. No wonder Christ's first parable has as its protagonist a sower whose planted seed promises a hundredfold harvest, or that his first miracle at Cana produces a flood of miraculous wine. As the Lord went about his ministry, he was struck by the certainty of the blind man who could not see Christ's presence but who pleaded for it all the same (see Mark 1:46–52).

Conversely, Christ was overcome by the way absence at the death of Lazarus devastated Lazarus's sisters Martha and Mary (see John 11:1–44). The onslaught of absence prompted Jesus to make Lazarus present again by bringing him back to life. That event anticipated the real presence of his Resurrection which Christ would offer the whole sorrowing world in the Eucharist. The faith of the centurion who declared, "Only say the word and my servant will be healed" (Matthew 8:8), assured Jesus that his believers were ready for an experience of his healing presence that transcends the restrictions of his physical attendance in a place. And when the solitary leper of the ten who had been cleansed returned to Jesus to offer him thanksgiving, the Lord was deeply moved (see Luke 17:11–19). Christ witnessed how powerfully the leper's act of thanksgiving completed his healing and restored his humanity. Perhaps at that moment the Lord resolved to leave us a graced way of offering thanks by which we can be perpetually made new. For the rest of his life, that cured leper lived out of the memory of the day that Jesus healed him; for him it was an event that never ended.

The memorial of the Eucharist remains a moving acknowledgment of Christ's presence that shapes the way we think, feel, act, and live. As we adore the Lord in the Blessed Sacrament, we pray that we may receive the Eucharistic imagination of Jesus whereby "our way of thinking is attuned to the Eucharist, and the Eucharist in turn confirms our way of thinking" (*CCC* 1327).

—PETER JOHN CAMERON, O.P.

A Thought for Reflection

Jesus was always centered on others and was devoted to supplying their needs—spiritual, physical, and emotional. What needs around you can you help to fill?

Oh Jesus, present in the Blessed Sacrament,

Give me your heart for others. Forgive me for my self-centeredness, and help me to be more aware of ways I can help others. It's only as you transform me by the grace of your presence that I can learn to think and act like you. Give me that grace always.

DECEMBER 20
Keeping a Journal

("Tim" answers questions from a Catholic journalist about his experience in Eucharistic Adoration.)

You mentioned earlier that you've kept a journal ever since you started with Adoration. Can you tell me about that?

I think it was my first Easter as a Catholic that I started using some of the time in Adoration for writing. Specifically, I began recording prayers. It started as a prayer journal, and it's become sort of an ongoing letter to Christ—prayers, petitions, praises, and just thoughts I've shared with him while in Adoration. It's been almost seven years now, and I've got all of it right here, in a three-ring binder. It's still growing strong, I guess you could say. It's interesting. When you said you'd be calling, I went back to look through some of the things I've written down. My spiritual odyssey through the years is laid out in all these pages. Most of it is too personal to publish, but it's helpful to me because sometimes it's easy to feel as though you haven't made much progress in your spiritual life, and this shows me otherwise. It provides real encouragement to persevere.

It's beautiful to go back and see where I was when I was still pretty new to the Catholic faith. And one of the things that really strikes me, when I go back and look at what I wrote down years ago, is that a lot of my big prayer requests have been answered. One of the things that's in there over and over again from those early years is a petition to God to grant me direction concerning my job. To look now and see the work I'm doing—using my writing skills for the Church— it's very clear that prayer has been answered. And those prayers for direction concerning my job have been replaced by other things on my mind and in my heart.

So many of my prayers, as I check back, have been answered. Of course, some haven't—or, at least, not in the way I was hoping for. And there are some things I see going all through these years that I'm sure I'll be praying for my whole life—the conversion of family members and things of that nature. But it really is awesome to see how many have been answered.

—QUOTED BY DAVID PEARSON

A Thought for Reflection

Have you ever kept a journal? It is a great help in remembering how God has answered your prayers and provided for your needs even before you thought to ask. Try taking a few minutes at the end of every day to write down all the blessings you have received that day, expressing your gratitude for them.

Oh Jesus, present in the Blessed Sacrament,

> Thank you for all the ways you have blessed me today. Thank you for hearing my prayers and answering them. Thank you for surprising me with your goodness. Let me always trust you for all I need.

DECEMBER 21
A Miracle

At the beginning of the eighth century, a priest was celebrating Mass at a monastery in Lanciano, Italy. Although he was reputed to be an intelligent and well-educated man, for some time he had been entertaining serious doubts regarding the real presence of Jesus in the Eucharist. When he spoke the words of Consecration at Mass on that particular day, he realized that the host was suddenly changed into a circle of flesh and that the wine in the chalice was transformed into blood. Weeping joyously, he invited those present to approach the altar to witness this miracle, and word quickly spread about this revelation.

The host and the blood have been carefully preserved over the centuries at the Church of the Miracle in Lanciano, and the church has been the site of pilgrimages ever since. Many studies of this miracle have been conducted, including one in 1970. This particular study was performed according to the strict guidelines that govern modern scientific research.

Scientists learned at that time that, even though the lunette containing the flesh was not hermetically sealed, the flesh was still intact and was identified as human muscular tissue from the heart wall, without any trace of any preservation agent. The blood type was AB. These scientists were amazed at the expert, tangential cut of the heart tissue—a cut that could only be made by someone who is intimately acquainted with human anatomy and who has extensive experience in dissection.

When they examined the blood, they noted it had not suffered from any spoilage, even though it was also kept over the centuries in a container not hermetically sealed. Normally blood is quickly altered through spoilage and decay. The blood was also found to be of human origin, and the same blood type as the flesh—AB.

Today, pilgrims to the Church of the Miracle in Lanciano can climb a staircase at the back of the altar to view the tabernacle and gaze upon the miraculous Eucharist in the reliquary. This miracle has continued for almost thirteen hundred years.

—John Hampsch, C.M.F.

A Thought for Reflection

God works miracles to increase our faith and to call attention to important truths. Many miracles have occurred over the years related to the Blessed Sacrament. Our response should be one of belief. What has helped to strengthen your faith in this sacrament?

Oh Jesus, present in the Blessed Sacrament,

> I believe in you; help my faith to grow stronger. Help me to appreciate the importance of this revelation, that your flesh is really my food and that your blood is really my drink. In these last few days before Christmas, help me to appreciate more than ever the fact of your presence near us.

DECEMBER 22
Spiritual Communion

A desire to be united to Jesus is the preeminent grace of the Eucharist. "In our inner life it is the Eucharist above all which expresses our personal union with Jesus…. The more perfectly we become assimilated to Christ in the Eucharist the more perfect will be our unity in him."[5]

Those who have mined the riches of Eucharistic treasure share that their lives are marked by a conscious anticipation for the Eucharist which is interwoven into the structure of the day. Often their minds turn toward the one whom they desire to receive. And, as their minds turn toward the sacramental presence of Jesus, flames of love stir the inner confines of their hearts. They experience an ever-increasing desire to be united to Jesus all of the time. This is the fruit of ardent desire, and it is produced by receiving Jesus in the sacrament with fervency and spiritual effectiveness.

This holy desire to be continuously united to Jesus flows from

5. Canon Jacques Leclercq, *The Interior Life,* trans. Fergus Murphy (New York: P.J. Kenedy & Sons, 1961), p. 88.

the Eucharistic presence into the soul that is properly disposed to receive him. We become one with him physically by receiving the host, and we become one with him spiritually—in mind, heart, and affection. For this reason, the Fathers of the Church made a distinction between a sacramental reception and a spiritual reception of the Sacrament.[6] This distinction has led to the holy practice of making a spiritual communion, an act of love prompted by the ardent desire to receive Holy Communion even when we cannot.

To make a spiritual communion, we simply unite ourselves with the one we love by fully turning our hearts and minds to him. Picturing him in his sacramental presence, viewing him with our mind's eye in the monstrance, remembering the moment we received him last— these are effective ways to direct our attention toward Jesus in the Eucharist. Then, we quietly tell him of our love. We may spontaneously speak to him from the fullness of our heart, or we may choose one of the formal prayers for spiritual communion. In either case, we experience abundant fruit from this act of love, and our hearts grow even warmer as we anticipate the next time we can receive Jesus sacramentally.

—Johnnette Benkovic

6. James T. O'Connor, *The Hidden Manna: A Theology of the Eucharist* (San Francisco: Ignatius, 1988), p. 322.

A Thought for Reflection

Activity levels really pick up as all the last-minute preparations for Christmas take place. In the midst of the hustle and bustle, make time for a spiritual communion and draw strength from those quiet moments with Jesus.

Oh Jesus, present in the Blessed Sacrament,

> I believe that you are in the Blessed Sacrament. I love you above all things, and I long for you in my soul. Since I cannot now receive you sacramentally, come at least spiritually into my heart. I embrace you as though you were already there and unite myself wholly to You. Never permit me to be separated from you.[7]

---

7. "An Act of Spiritual Communion," *EWTN*, https://www.ewtn.com/Devotionals/prayers/blsac4.htm.

DECEMBER 23
Prepare to Receive Jesus

So, let's ask ourselves some questions about how we can prepare ourselves to receive Communion most effectively. How can we maximize our openness to all forms of healing through this sacrament? How do we advance more and more in our spiritual lives, thereby experiencing greater spiritual healing? How do we prepare ourselves for our emotional healing, so that all the various facets of our personalities might be better integrated? How do we prepare ourselves for our physical healing so that our bodies might be healed while receiving the Body of Christ in the Eucharist? How do we incorporate ourselves more perfectly in a societal or communitarian dimension into the mystical Body of Christ?

According to St. Alphonsus Liguori, we can prepare ourselves. He tells us we can do this by being detached from creatures and by driving from our hearts everything that is not of God and for God. He emphasizes this point by telling a story from the life of St. Gertrude. St. Gertrude asked our Lord what preparation he required of her for Holy Communion. He replied, "I only ask that you come empty of yourself to receive me." What does this mean? It means that everything that captures our attention must be directly or indirectly related to God. If something becomes an end in itself, then it distracts us from God. For example, television might not be outrightly evil, but it certainly can become a distraction. Today especially, TV has a great potential for instilling a worldly spirit within us. St. Alphonsus recognized that a worldly spirit, in general, is always assailing us. Even though the harried, preoccupied soul may be in a state of grace and, therefore, still be God's friend, the heart can be so overtaken by a worldly spirit there is no room to grow in divine love. We need to detach ourselves from any worldly spirit that does not have a direct relationship with God (see 1 John 3:7–10).

—John Hampsch, C.M.F.

A Thought for Reflection

God's revelation to St. Gertrude was that he wanted her to be empty in order to receive him. How can you empty yourself? What obstacles keep you from receiving the Eucharist with peace and devotion?

Oh Jesus, present in the Blessed Sacrament,

The Church grows silent as our attention is focused on Bethlehem. All is ready for your birth, and we wait in peace for your coming to us as a tiny baby. Prepare my heart for the wonder of your coming, both in the mystery of the Incarnation and in the mystery of the Eucharist.

DECEMBER 24
Self-Emptying Love

Eucharistic devotion is not magical, because magic implies control and manipulation, power over things. Nor is it a focus on externals, since it takes me to the threshold of the external and the internal and integrates them. The exposed Blessed Sacrament is not an object but a person who is infinitely self-emptying love, giving himself, pouring himself out right before our eyes and right into us.

To adore our Lord in the Blessed Sacrament requires falling to my knees, realizing how small I am. Even more, it requires going out in faith and in smallness, offering myself to him who offers himself to me. The Incarnation is sometimes defined as a marvelous exchange whereby God shares in our humanity in order to give us a share in his divinity. The Eucharist allows us to embody this marvelous exchange.

As we assimilate what all this means, how could our disposition be any other than adoration? This is interpersonal communication of the most intimate kind, offered by God and received by us in total powerlessness.

One day near the end of Pope John Paul II's life, one of his aides found him sitting in his altar chair in his private chapel. He had his arms around the tabernacle and was singing in Polish. The aide left the chapel but later asked the pope what he had been doing. Pope John Paul responded that he had been singing a song his mother used to sing to him as a boy when he was sad. He had been comforting our Lord.[8]

This marvelous exchange that the Lord initiates flows both ways if we are small enough to allow this intimacy and not be afraid of its passion. Let us take opportunities to contemplate this in the fullest sense, participating in the very life of him whom we have received.

—THOMAS ACKLIN, O.S.B.

A THOUGHT FOR REFLECTION

O holy night! Tonight our dear Savior is born! With shepherds and angels, we go to Bethlehem to worship the newborn king. Our God is with us. Heaven and earth sing for joy, and our hearts join in the chorus.

8. Robert Reilly, "Fearless: How John Paul II Changed the Political World," *Crisis*, May 2005, p. 27.

Oh Jesus, present in the Blessed Sacrament,

The heavens ring out with shouts of joy as the angels announce your coming. I join my song to that of the angels and proclaim the miracle of your birth. Glory to God in the highest, and on earth peace among men with whom he is pleased! Alleluia!

DECEMBER 25
The Birth of Jesus

The star over the stable was the first sanctuary lamp. By its light, angels, shepherds and kings were drawn to Bethlehem, the "House of Bread," to adore God with us. In the presence of a baby, even the most hardhearted person changes and becomes tender and caring. But there is an even greater exceptionality about this newborn. "For in him all things were created, in heaven and on earth…. In him all the fulness of God was pleased to dwell" (Colossians 1:16, 19). In the presence of the infant Jesus, we recognize what corresponds exactly to the deepest longings of our hearts. Everything that we have been looking for has become flesh and is now lying in this manger. We were made for this presence. All my life my "I" has been waiting to adore this "You." To Christ we say: The fullness of my being is you; my meaning is you. Every time I adore the Blessed Sacrament, Jesus attracts my heart anew.

—PETER JOHN CAMERON, O.P.

Emmanuel, God with Us

Now the birth of Jesus Christ took place in this way. When his mother Mary had been betrothed to Joseph, before they came together she was found to be with child of the Holy Spirit; and her husband Joseph, being a just man and unwilling to put her to shame, resolved to send her away quietly. But as he considered this, behold, an angel of the Lord appeared to him in a dream, saying, "Joseph, son of David, do not fear to take Mary your wife, for that which is conceived in her is of the Holy Spirit; she will bear a son, and you shall call his name Jesus, for he will save his people from their sins." All this took place to fulfil what the Lord had spoken by the prophet:

"Behold, a virgin shall conceive and bear a son,
and his name shall be called Emmanuel"
(which means, God with us).
—Matthew 1:18–23

A Thought for Reflection

Take a few minutes to reflect on the reason for our celebration and joy today and to thank Jesus for coming to us. It will make all the other celebrations that much more joyful.

Oh Jesus, present in the Blessed Sacrament,

How humbly you have come, yet how great is your coming! My Lord and my God, I adore you!

DECEMBER 26
Mary's Praise

O ne element that should characterize our thanksgiving after Communion is praise. Jesus is present within us in the temples of our hearts. We are carrying Jesus, the incarnate Son of God, in our hearts. Songs of praise and rejoicing should welcome him. As an example, we need only to recall Mary's song of praise and rejoicing when she was carrying Jesus in her womb:

> My soul magnifies the Lord,
> and my spirit rejoices in God my Savior,
> for he has regarded the low estate of his handmaiden.
> For behold, henceforth all generations will call me blessed;
> for he who is mighty has done great things for me,
> and holy is his name. (Luke 1:46–49)

Although nothing in Mary's outward appearance distinguished her from other pregnant women, in the depths of her heart she was living out the closest possible union between God and one of his creatures.

She was a living tabernacle where the Holy of Holies was residing. Unceasingly she prayed that she might adore the Word made flesh within her, that she might be united more closely with God and be transformed by his love, and that she might join in offering continual praise, which is the only homage worthy of the almighty and omnipotent God. When we receive the living Jesus into our hearts at Holy Communion, we too become temples of the living God and share in this prayer of Mary. We should strive to live in this spirit of continual adoration of the Trinity dwelling within our souls.

We have a lot to look forward to! Through the Eucharist, Jesus is giving us a foretaste of the banquet he has prepared for us in heaven. Are we enjoying it, or are we simply skipping through it? Are we simply blundering our way through all these precious treasures? Are we appreciative and thankful for God's gift to us? Are we bursting with gratitude for this greatest of gifts?

—JOHN HAMPSCH, C.M.F.

A THOUGHT FOR REFLECTION

Mary rejoiced because "he who is mighty has done great things for me." Make a list of the wonderful things God has done for you and spend some time in joyful thanksgiving.

Oh Jesus, present in the Blessed Sacrament,

With joy in my heart and in a spirit of gratitude, I thank you for your great blessings in my life. Thank you for the celebration of your birth. Thank you for restoring my hope of eternal life with you. Thank you for all the gifts I have received from your generous hand.

DECEMBER 27
"Eat My Flesh and Drink My Blood"

The Blessed Eucharist is *the* Sacrament. Baptism exists for it, all the others are enriched by it. The whole being is nourished by it. It is precisely food, which explains why it is the one sacrament meant to be received daily. Without it, one petition in the Our Father—"Give us this day our daily bread"—lacks the fullness of its meaning.

Early in his ministry, as St. John tells us (see chapter 6), our Lord gave the first promise of it. He had just worked what is probably the most famous of his miracles, the feeding of the five thousand. The next day, in the synagogue at Capernaum on the shore of the Sea of Galilee, our Lord made a speech which should be read and reread. Here we quote a few phrases: "He that eats my flesh and drinks my blood has eternal life; and I will raise him up at the last day. For my flesh is food indeed; and my blood is drink indeed. He who eats my flesh, and drinks my blood, abides in me, and I in him"; "He that eats me shall live because of me."

He saw that many of his own disciples were horrified at what he was saying. We know what he meant: In saying they must eat his flesh, he did not mean dead flesh but his body with the life in it, with the living soul in it. In some way he himself, living, was to be the food of their soul's life. Needless to say, all this meant nothing whatever to those who heard it first. For many, it was the end of discipleship. They simply left him, probably thinking that for a man to talk of giving them his flesh to eat was mere insanity. When he asked the apostles if they would go too, Peter gave him one of the most moving answers in all man's history: "Lord, to whom shall we go?" He had not the faintest idea what it all meant, but he had a total belief in the Master he had chosen and simply hoped that someday it would be made plain.

—FRANK SHEED

A THOUGHT FOR REFLECTION

For almost a month you have been learning about Jesus's presence in the Blessed Sacrament, both through reading and prayer. How has your attitude about the Blessed Sacrament changed? Today he asks if you will stay with him, or walk away with the rest of the crowd. What is your response?

Oh Jesus, present in the Blessed Sacrament,

I have only begun to know you, and I realize how much more there is to know. Draw me closer to you every day. As I look forward to the coming year, I ask for a deeper hunger to eat your Body and drink your Blood.

The One We Are Looking For

THE PRESENTATION OF THE LORD

One of the high points of the Easter Vigil liturgy is the moment after Holy Communion when the Blessed Sacrament is reposed in the tabernacle. Since the end of the Mass of the Lord's Supper on Holy Thursday night, the tabernacle has lain empty and open—bare and abandoned. But now—once again—the "glory of the Lord fills the temple" (see Ezekiel 43:5). The return of the Eucharistic Lord to the tabernacle mimics in a way the moment when the presence of Christ fills the temple at the Presentation of the Lord. The Presentation confirms that Jesus is the firstborn Son who belongs to the Lord. In this mystery Jesus offers us a share in that belonging. God answers our heartfelt cry for meaning, not with mere words, but with a presence in the arms of Mary. What formerly was barren and abandoned in our life is now filled with that presence.

Finding Jesus in the Temple

The time when Jesus goes missing prepares us for the days when Jesus will be in the tomb as well as for the days after the Ascension. It is not until Jesus is lost from our sight that we realize how radically our life has been changed because of his presence. Our Communion with Christ has confirmed a truth that we cannot deny: In order to be myself, I need someone else, for alone I cannot be myself. Why? Because when I become conscious of myself right to my very core, I perceive there at the depths of the self, an other. And I belong to this other. My belonging to this other who dwells in my depths precedes any sense of solitude or loneliness I may feel. I was made to be with him. He is the one I am looking for as I search for the missing Jesus. I find him in the temple, in the tabernacle, being about his Father's business.

—Peter John Cameron, O.P.

A Thought for Reflection

The more we study the life of Jesus, the more we see that everything in his life was designed to draw us close to him. The more we read about his life, the more we can connect to him today. Reading the Gospel for each day is a wonderful way to connect to Jesus. What is he saying to you today through the stories of his life?

Oh Jesus, present in the Blessed Sacrament,

Help me to know you a little bit more every day. Send me your Holy Spirit so I can understand the meaning of the Gospels and meet you in your Word, as I meet you in the Blessed Sacrament. I open my heart to all the ways you want to speak to me.

December 29
More of Jesus, Less of Me

The Eucharist is infinitely more than just a symbol, or memory of a pious meal. Christ in this sacrament is real and present. The living, tangible, flesh and blood presence of Jesus in the Eucharist commits us to the poor and wounded of our world. Their hunger and thirst must become our hunger and thirst. Only a whole civilization of love can provide for these kinds of needs. The engine by which such a civilization can be built is the liturgy, which is the source and summit of God's love for us. Only the love that comes from God and goes to God is powerful enough to heal the wounds of our brothers and sisters, in this and every age. If we truly believe in the real presence of Christ in the Eucharist, and we act on it, then others will clearly see and want the joy that is ours. If we enter more deeply into the solidarity of love that the Holy Spirit offers us in the liturgy, then God will use us to sanctify the world.

As believers, our task in the liturgy involves working to recover the right focus and the proper reverence in our worship. The Mass is not a show, or a performance, or a kind of entertainment. The Eucharist is about God. It should focus that worship and our hearts where they belong—on him, not on us. We're important, because Jesus died for us, but we're secondary in the act of worship. Thus, our musicians, liturgists, acolytes, lectors, and extraordinary ministers of Holy Communion—all the wonderful people who serve in these roles—need to become transparent, humble, and deeply faithful to the liturgy that the Church defines so that nothing distracts us from our encounter with God.

The more unselfish we are, the greater the work that Jesus will accomplish through us. In the liturgy and in our lives of service we need to become less so that Jesus will become more. We need to become invisible, so that God will become ever more visible.

—CHARLES J. CHAPUT, O.F.M. CAP.

A THOUGHT FOR REFLECTION

Devotion to the Eucharist makes us see the world in a different way. We start to see things through Jesus's eyes, and he begins to live his life through us. We become more like him. Pray for the grace to humbly surrender your will, so that God's will can be done through you.

Oh Jesus, present in the Blessed Sacrament,

I rejoice to know you on a deeper level. Show me where my stubborn will gets in your way. Let me be a pure channel through which your grace can flow to others.

December 30
He Will Indeed Refresh Us

It is wonderful that many parishes have begun to have perpetual Adoration of the Blessed Sacrament, exposed in the monstrance, over the past twenty-five years. However, most Eucharistic holy hours, including those of the saints and Bishop Sheen have been made not before the monstrance but before the tabernacle. Although it is a great privilege to pray before the monstrance, praying before the tabernacle is also a great privilege and we should take advantage of this when exposure is not available.

Some may ask, "What would I do during an hour of prayer?" Well, here are some possibilities. Meditate on Sacred Scripture, especially the readings for the next day's Mass, meditate on the mysteries of the rosary, make the Stations of the Cross, pray the Liturgy of the Hours. Or you might just do as a parishioner of St. John Vianney did during his many hours before the Blessed Sacrament, "I look at the good Lord, and he looks at me."[9]

9. See Francis Trochu, *The Curé d'Ars: St. Jean-Marie Baptiste Vianney*, trans. Dom Ernest Graf (Rockford, Ill.: TAN, 1977), p. 184.

Why should you pray before the Blessed Sacrament as opposed to some other place? The saints should inspire us. St. Francis of Assisi, it seems, was the first to go and pray in churches where the Blessed Sacrament was reserved for the sick. St. Clare spent long hours in prayer before the Blessed Sacrament, and her face would glow when she came out. St. John of the Cross slept only two or three hours a night because he was praying before the Blessed Sacrament. His face also shone with brightness at times.

Pope John Paul II is said to have spent two hours a day before the Blessed Sacrament in prayer, and Blessed Mother Teresa of Calcutta and her nuns spent three hours a day there. What better way to do as Our Lord has asked, "Come to me, all who labor and are heavy laden, and I will give you rest" (Matthew 11:28).

He will indeed refresh us!

—Thomas G. Morrow

....

A Thought for Reflection

As we come to the end of a busy season and a busy year, Jesus promises to refresh us and give us his rest. As you think about making resolutions for the year ahead, is more time with Jesus in the Blessed Sacrament on your list? He wants to refresh you next year.

....

Oh Jesus, present in the Blessed Sacrament,

Sometimes I think of prayer as a duty, but you have shown me that it is a time of renewal, peace, and refreshment. You carry my burdens for me. Thank you for opening my eyes to your goodness and restorative grace. May I be still before you and soak in your love.

December 31
Persevere

. . . .

This touches upon another objection some make to Eucharistic Devotion: that it makes us too introspective, too individualistic in our relationship with God, thus less likely to face the real challenges of life and relationships with others. But we need never fear that allowing ourselves to be alone with Jesus will lead us to a self-centered spirituality of "me and Jesus," that we will forget our neighbor and the community, especially those who are most in need. The director of spiritual life at one seminary noted that the seminarians who voluntarily spent time in the chapel adoring the sacrament each day were the ones who signed up to help out at the food bank and at the homeless men's mission.

Prayer and any relationship requires time. This is the meaning of the classical devotion of the "holy hour." Though Jesus reproached his disciples for not being able to stay awake and pray with him one hour (see Matthew 26:40–46), there is nothing magical about sixty minutes except that it suggest an extended time to allow things to happen, to allow the love of the one we have received to penetrate us.

It is nearly impossible for some of us to sit still long enough to try this, which only demonstrates how urgent the need is to do it.

As anyone who has tried to pray in this way knows, if one perseveres and remains, the romantic glow fades. Faith is even tested as we wonder if this is all a hoax, if there is nothing here but bread, if we are wasting time in this church all by ourselves. Ideas about things we could be doing and other distractions can besiege us as we try to concentrate in prayer.

Anyone who has been through the experience of living out a committed relationship, undertaking serious study or research, learning a language or how to play a musical instrument or a new game knows similar doubts and fears. Just as many in our times do not persevere long enough to see what happens if they remain in that troubled marriage, many do not enter deeply enough into prayer to outlast the dryness, the distractions, the doubts. Consequently they never get very deeply into a relationship with our Lord and never develop much interiority.

How should we persevere? The main thing we need to do is to simply stay there and prolong the prayer and devotion we had at the moment we received the Eucharist.

—THOMAS ACKLIN, O.S.B.

A Thought for Reflection

Perseverance is a key to making any long-lasting change in life. Most New Year's resolutions last only a few weeks. How can you persevere in your devotion to the Blessed Sacrament in the year ahead? Make a plan for daily prayer, and ask Jesus for help to stick with it.

Oh Jesus, present in the Blessed Sacrament,

I am full of gratitude that you have taught me about your real presence and the joy that comes from spending time with you. Give me the grace to be faithful, because the most important thing in my life is to surrender to you and know you better. Teach me to serve others—to give my time and resources to those in need. Let me lose myself and find you.

JANUARY 1

The Fruit of Mary's Womb

St. Irenaeus once said that anyone who does not comprehend God's birth of Mary cannot comprehend the Eucharist either. And this makes sense. For, weighed down as we are by the effects of original sin, our tendency is to turn God and faith into an abstraction. The concreteness of the Eucharist is given to us precisely to prevent us from that error. And it all begins when God takes on real, human flesh in the womb of Mary, the Mother of God.

Fr. Raniero Cantalamessa reminds us that the Latin for "mother"—*mater*—comes from the word *materia* (matter/material). He says that by silently entering the womb of a woman, God comes down into the very heart of matter, concretely and "really." And the God who became flesh in a woman's womb is the same God who comes to us in the heart of matter which is the Eucharist. Moreover, as Pope John Paul II pointed out, not only does Mary lead us to Christ, but also Christ leads us to his Mother. As the *Catechism* expresses it, "Mary's function as mother of men in no way obscures or diminishes [the] unique mediation of Christ, but rather shows its power" (*CCC* 970, quoting *Lumen Gentium*, 60).

I heard a story about a woman named Cheryl Carter-Shotts decided to adopt a young African orphan named Mohammed after learning about his plight while watching television. When the complicated process was at last completed, Mohammed did not understand the concept of adoption; he thought he was being brought to the United States to become the woman's servant. Shocked at this, Cheryl said, "I don't want you to be my houseboy; I want you to be my son." The boy replied: "I don't know what that means...but if you teach me, I will learn."

Christ leads us to his Mother so that through her maternal mediation we will learn what it means to become God's sons, God's daughters. She leads us to the Fruit of her womb—the Eucharistic Jesus—whereby we become truly his brothers and sisters. St. John Vianney says that after the Lord had given us all he could—his Body and Blood to be food for our souls—he willed also to give us the most precious thing he had left, which was his holy Mother. One gift leads to the other.

—PETER JOHN CAMERON, O.P.

A Thought for Reflection

The Church sets aside January 1 as a day to honor Mary, the Mother of God. In a special way Mary leads us closer to her Son in Eucharistic Adoration. Ask for her intercession that your faith in her Son, Jesus, will be strengthened this year.

Oh Jesus, present in the Blessed Sacrament,

> Bring me closer to your Mother, who in turn will bring me close to you. Mary, as your child I rely on your motherly prayers. Your whole life was devoted to making Jesus known and loved. Pray for me to love him more this year than ever before.

How Have You Changed?

("Mal" answers questions from a Catholic journalist about his experience in Eucharistic Adoration.)

What difference does Eucharistic Adoration make in your life?

If Jesus didn't make himself available for me to be close to in this way, I think my faith would be much more superficial. He challenges me when I go in there. You can't very well sit in Jesus's presence hour after hour, week after week, and tell him how much you love him, how much you want to follow him and be close to him and change for him—and then go and casually commit all kinds of little sins. You go and do what you told him you would do. He might be telling me, "You need to work on your anger." Or this needs to be worked on or that needs to be worked on. And I see his tremendous humility and love, coming to me in such a humble way—under the appearance of plain, man-made bread—and know that he is calling me to the same kind of humility and love. And that's most especially what I've gotten through Eucharistic Adoration: humility. As a side benefit, I've also gotten a sense of spiritual progress. It's been slow but sure.

What makes you so sure you're in the actual, physical presence of Jesus when you're before the Blessed Sacrament?

The effect it has on me. I am becoming more like him whom I am adoring. If that's not Jesus under the appearance of bread, as my faith and two thousand years of Church teaching tell me, then why am I being transformed so radically? Is a piece of bread making me into something I'm not? If that's not Jesus Christ up there, I can't explain how or why a person who was filled with selfish longing, anger, hate, rage, jealousy, envy—you name a vice, I had it in spades—is becoming the person you're talking to. Someone who now knows what love and peace and tranquility are. My eyes are opened; my heart is new. You'll have to trust me when I tell you, because you didn't know me before: What you see in me is radical transformation. And it's Jesus's doing, not mine.

—QUOTED BY DAVID PEARSON

A Thought for Reflection

Mal found his faith and humility strengthened through his time of Eucharistic Adoration. What changes have you seen in yourself? What do you think Jesus wants you to learn as you move ahead?

Oh Jesus, present in the Blessed Sacrament,

> Every day as I spend time with you I see myself changing. Even my struggles have new meaning, as I experience your help and strength in the midst of difficulties. Let me become more like you each day. Forgive my sins, and set me free to love and serve you and those around me.

JANUARY 3
A Tremendous Privilege

To prepare ourselves to receive the Body and Blood of Jesus, St. Alphonsus recommends we stir up "a great desire to receive Jesus Christ and his holy love," with a view of advancing in divine love. We should take great care that we do not go to Communion as just another act within the ceremony of the Mass. We should see it as the tremendous privilege it is, rather than as an obligation. We should desire to receive Jesus with a view to loving him more and advancing in love of God. If fervent love is not present, then something is drastically missing. We should frequently ask ourselves whether the component of love is present in our relationship with Jesus, and most especially in the sacrament of love, the Holy Eucharist.

Looking again at St. Alphonsus's words that "only those who are famishing will receive their fill at this sacred banquet," let us be aware that the ones who are really satisfied, who feel enriched, and who experience healing in their lives are those who truly hunger and yearn for Jesus and not for healing in itself. Remember the blind man who called out, "Jesus, Son of David, have mercy on me." He did not call out, "Jesus, come and heal my blindness." First he acknowledged Jesus as the Messiah. First he sought the Healer. He sought the healing only after Jesus asked him, "What do you want?" We too have to seek the Healer before we seek the healing.

This can be difficult for many people. When people suffer, it is so easy for them to become preoccupied with the pain or with the urgency of the problem. As a result, they focus on the physical, emotional, or spiritual healing and forget about giving glory to God. We need to be sure that our priorities are right. Jesus was a man of great priorities: "Seek *first* his kingdom and his righteousness, and all these things shall be yours as well" (Matthew 6:33, emphasis added). We need to focus primarily on Jesus as a person in the Eucharist, and only then approach him with our own needs, such as healing.

—JOHN HAMPSCH, C.M.F.

A THOUGHT FOR REFLECTION

Today we are reminded to come to Holy Communion with a hunger for the gift of God. We find many ways to distract ourselves from our true spiritual hunger. Our culture offers so much noise that keeps us from acknowledging the central place Jesus should have in our hearts.

What distracts you? How can you prepare to receive the Eucharist more reflectively?

Oh Jesus, present in the Blessed Sacrament,

Make me ready to receive you in Holy Communion. I never want to take you for granted or be complacent about your gift to me. Forgive my sins so I can receive you worthily. I turn my focus to your love, your truth, and your promises. Thank you for the gift I am about to receive. Feed me with the food that satisfies the deepest desires of my heart.

JANUARY 4
Say Thank You

J ust as we should devote adequate time to preparing our hearts before receiving Holy Communion, St. Alphonsus also advises us to spend adequate time in thanksgiving afterward. He observes that "no prayer is more dear to God than that which is made after Holy Communion."

Other saints have also stressed the importance of devoting adequate time to thanksgiving after Communion. St. John Chrysostom noted that when we enjoy a delicious meal at a banquet, we savor every morsel and refuse anything bitter afterward so we will not lose the sweet flavor of the food we so thoroughly enjoyed. He advises us, therefore, to take great care not to lose the heavenly flavor of the Body of Jesus Christ by turning to the cares of the world too soon.

What, then, constitutes a good thanksgiving? We should complete our union with Jesus by sincerely offering ourselves to him. Nothing can be more intimate than the union that takes place between the Creator and his creatures in Communion. The immense love that

Jesus has for us should be the focus of our attention. But Jesus's love for us should evoke, in turn, our love for him. Love must be mutual to produce union. We must return love for love.

The second element of our thanksgiving after Communion is a time of petition. Our first and foremost petition should be that God will grant us the grace to fulfill everything we have promised to him in offering ourselves to him. At the same time, we can really take advantage of—in a good sense—the beneficence of Jesus in our soul. As St. Teresa reminds us, he is there as a king reigning in our hearts, offering to grant us whatever we seek that conforms with his will.

We need to remember this when we receive him in Holy Communion. He is present within us and is asking us, "What do you want?" This is a time to give Jesus our love and our faith. To trust him. To ask him what we want to ask him and let him heal us. Indeed, Jesus wants more for us than we want for ourselves!

—JOHN HAMPSCH, C.M.F.

A THOUGHT FOR REFLECTION

If we truly understood the wonder of the gift we receive, we would never stop thanking God for the Eucharist. Pray for a grateful heart. Practice gratitude every day, and it will become a habit of your heart.

Oh Jesus, present in the Blessed Sacrament,

Thank you for calling me by name and revealing your love to me. Thank you for the gift of my faith. Thank you for teaching me about this wonderful sacrament. Thank you for providing all my needs and for the people in my life who remind me of your goodness. Thank you for coming to me.

January 5
What We Need, Not What We Want

("Diane" answers questions from a Catholic journalist about her experience in Eucharistic Adoration.)

So your time before the Blessed Sacrament is deeply quiet, and it lets you feel God's love.

Yes. But I also think it lets you look around and get down to a level that you can see what you really need. And I mean need, as opposed to what's nice to have. We're surrounded by all these material things and we're not above all that just because we go to Eucharistic Adoration, just because we really try to live our Christian faith. We're still tempted by the modern world's comforts, conveniences, and diversions.

Everybody wants to have nice things for their family. But at the same time, it's easier to sort through that stuff and separate them from the things that are God-given. You can find beauty in non-materialistic things around you that you never much noticed before. Circumstances, people, opportunities to be there for people going through various kinds of struggles. I mean, you look around and you think, "Do I really need the new clothes, the new car, whatever?" And you find the strength to say, "No, that's not going to make me happy." You can see past the selling, the pitch. I actually find myself more tuned in to all the natural beauty around me. Not to sound corny, but I mean like in simple leaves on the trees in our yard or the flowers I have in my plants. I find that I appreciate the smaller things like those much more now than I used to. Is that appreciation flowing from my deeper faith, from my time spent with Jesus in Eucharistic Adoration? I honestly don't know. Maybe it's just me getting older. But I do know that, in my quiet time before the Blessed Sacrament, I thank God for my growing appreciation of these little things; I'm aware of my diminishing appetite for the material things that used to seem so important and irresistible. God's real presence brings me back to his grace, back to the simple things in life being enough.

—QUOTED BY DAVID PEARSON

A THOUGHT FOR REFLECTION

Time spent in Adoration tends to clarify our priorities. Possessions become less important and spiritual treasure begins to capture our hearts. Are you holding on to things that get in the way of a humble surrender to Jesus? He wants to be everything for you.

Oh Jesus, present in the Blessed Sacrament,

You are my treasure. Your life is all that truly satisfies the deepest part of me. Help me to let go of everything else so you can be first in my mind and my heart. Thank you for this awesome invitation.

January 6
Now What?

I sincerely hope and pray that, in hearing accounts of ordinary folks living lives of extraordinary closeness to Christ, you too will be moved to give Jesus a chance to work in your life through Eucharistic Adoration.

Where to go to meet our Lord in his humanity as well as his divinity? Many parishes offer perpetual Adoration or set times of Adoration throughout the week. If you find that there are no Adoration opportunities near you, you can still visit with Jesus. While the term "Eucharistic Adoration" is formally used to describe prayer before the exposed Host, you can obtain the exact same graces and spiritual benefits by visiting the Lord wherever the Blessed Sacrament is reserved in a tabernacle. And that's the case in nearly every Catholic Church.

In fact, for me personally, it was by praying before the Blessed Sacrament reserved in a tabernacle in a nearby parish church, just a few minutes of my lunch break each weekday, that I heard God prompting me, quietly but firmly, to leave my job in the secular media for a position in the Catholic press.

No matter how you choose to spend your time with Jesus while you sit with him, be assured that, over time, if you are faithful in your visits, your life will change. You will change. As you do, you may find it helpful to know that, in Adoration, you're practicing an ancient form of devotion known as contemplative prayer.

Among Eucharistic adorers, the story is often told of St. John Vianney, the small, humble and holy pastor of a country parish in Ars, France, in the 1800s. Fr. Vianney, who would come to be known as the Curé of Ars, used to watch a farmer coming into the church after working the fields late each afternoon. Day after day, the farmer would kneel and pray before the Blessed Sacrament. Finally Fr. Vianney, eager to progress in his own prayer life, asked the farmer what it was that he was saying to God each day. "Oh, I don't say anything," the farmer told him. "I look at him, and he looks at me."

That's contemplative prayer. That's Eucharistic Adoration. That's interior transformation. And that's love—the most essential personal project you can take upon yourself if you're serious about pitching in to help build the kingdom of God.

I hope to see you there.

—David Pearson

A Thought for Reflection

Jesus waits for you and hopes to spend more time with you. He hopes to draw you into a marvelous love through his living presence in the Blessed Sacrament. He is with you, close to you.

O Jesus, present in the Blessed Sacrament,

> My joy, my treasure, my deep desire, my Lord, and my God, thank you for this journey of knowledge and union. It is a journey that never ends. Help me to start anew every day to give myself to you, as you always give yourself to me. Amen.

SOURCES

As indicated, all reflections for this book were drawn from books published by Servant Books. To find any of these titles, please visit our catalog at www.FranciscanMedia.org.

Acklin, Thomas, O.S.B. *The Passion of the Lamb: The Self-Giving Love of Jesus* (December 4, 24, 31)

Apostoli, Fr. Andrew, C.F.R. *Walk Humbly With Your God: Simple Steps to a Virtuous Life* (December 3, 11, 13, 16)

Aquilina, Mike. *Fire of God's Love: 120 Reflections on the Eucharist* (December 2)

Benkovic, Johnnette. *Full of Grace: Women and the Abundant Life* (December 5, 17, 22)

Cameron, Father Peter John, O.P. *Jesus, Present Before Me: Meditations for Eucharistic Adoration* (December 1, 8, 19, 25, 28; January 1)

Chaput, Charles J., O.F.M. Cap. *Living the Catholic Faith: Rediscovering the Basics* (December 29)

Hampsch, John, C.M.F. *The Healing Power of the Eucharist* (December 7, 9, 10, 15, 21, 23, 26; January 3, 4)

Magee, Peter. *God's Mercy Revealed: Healing for a Broken World* (December 6, 12)

Morrow, Fr. Thomas G. *Be Holy: A Catholic's Guide to the Spiritual Life* (December 30)

Pearson, David. *No Wonder They Call it the Real Presence: Lives Changed in Eucharistic Adoration* (December 18, 20; January 2, 5, 6)

Sheed, Frank. *Theology for Beginners* (December 27)